FIFTEEN WALKS FROM
PATTERDALE AND ULLSWATER

PAUL BUTTLE

Published by
amadorn

I would like to thank the following people
for the help they have given me in producing this guide:
Jill Preston, Pat Clark, Lynne Denny,
Hilary Drummond, Tom Gleason
agus Pádraig Ciobháin arís.

First published May, 1992
Reprinted October, 1992

ISBN 0 9519345 0 3

Published by Amadorn, 18 Brewery Lane, Keswick, Cumbria.
Printed by Nuffield Press, Oxford.

CONTENTS

INTRODUCTION

The fifteen walks in this guide present a wide choice from modest low level walks to very challenging high level walks. Probably not all the walks will be of interest to every walker, but hopefully every walker will find six or seven that are.

Order of Walks

I have ordered the walks, at least within each category; low, intermediate and high level, as much as I could judge, by the amount of effort involved. Thus the easiest walks come first in the guide and the hardest last. This ordering of the walks I hope will serve some purpose in helping you to decide which one to choose.

Timing of the walks

This is always difficult to judge as it depends not only on an individual's fitness but also on their predilection for sitting down every now and then. The 'suggested times' in this book therefore are just a rough guide. They are calculated on the basis of allowing one hour for every three miles and an hour for every thousand feet of ascent and then, in most cases, rounded up to the nearest hour. This way of calculating the time a walk will take however does not allow for any stops or picnics. If you are therefore prone to making a lot of stops to admire the scenery or to consume food or to compose some great epic verse you should adapt the suggested times accordingly.

Choice of maps.

A map is essential on the fells and even on low level walks it is best to be with one. The Ordnance Survey produce three different scale maps that can be used in conjunction with this guide:-

The 'One Inch' Tourist Map of the Lake District, scale 1:63,360.

Of all the Lake District maps this is definitely the best value for money in that it covers the whole area of the Lake District. I have done practically all of my walking in the Lake District using this map. However for low level walks it is not the best map to navigate by as it lacks any representation of field boundaries. In addition, unfortunately, in recent years the Ordnance Survey have done their best to spoil the aesthetic appeal and durability of this map by covering it with ghastly purple splodges and by printing it on ridiculously thin paper. Worse still, and this is an act of pure vandalism, they have 'metricated' the contours. The virtue of the 1:63,360 scale is that one inch represents one mile. Just how many people are there who visualise distances in miles but heights in metres? Well, quite a few it would seem in the Ordnance Survey.

Landranger series sheet 90, scale 1:50,000.

This is a true metric map. 2 cm represents one kilometre, which is also the size of the grid squares. So if you do think in metric this is an excellent map. All the walks in this guide are covered by this map, and although it is drawn to a scale which is only slightly larger than the Tourist Map it is surprisingly clearer. Its one drawback is that it does not cover the whole of the Lake District.

Outdoor Leisure Map Sheet 5, English Lakes - North Eastern area, scale 1:25,000

This is an amazingly detailed map. All the walks in this guide are covered by this map. As it shows all field boundaries, stone walls and fences etc., it is definitely the best map to use for low level walks. Its one fault is the way in which it represents footpaths. At first sight this would seem clear enough, footpaths are represented by bold green dashed lines. They are not, or at least not always. The green dashed lines are rights of way; in some places, most places, a footpath or a bridleway does indeed follow the right of way, but in other places there might be no footpath at all following the right of way or it might be a hundred yards or more away. Real existing footpaths are represented on the map as feint black dashed lines, which you have to look very closely to see. Their representation of actual existing footpaths though is remarkably accurate and suprisingly comprehensive.

Public Transport

Using public transport it is possible to reach the starting point of all the walks in this guide from either Penrith or Windermere, and all places in between along the A592 at least during the summer. Outside the summer season connections are limited to those places between Patterdale and Penrith. The three transport services which provide these connections are:-

Bus. Service 108. Operators Cumberland Motor Services.

This runs from Penrith to the Patterdale Hotel via Pooley Bridge and Glenridding. In summer extends to Windermere via Hartsop along the A592. For enquiries Tel. Carlisle (0228) 48484.

Postbus. Penrith to Martindale.

The sevice extends to St. Martin's church. For pick up times look at the post boxes or Tel. Penrith (0768) 62708

Ullswater Motoryacht.

Three daily sailings between Glenridding, Howtown and Pooley Bridge from April to November. For Enquiries Tel. Kendal (0539) 721 626 or Glenridding (076 84) 82229

Safety

Most of the walks in this guide are serious high level fell walks. Make sure therefore you are properly equipped if you go on them, as weather conditions on the fell tops can be radically different from those in the valleys.

Tá an gleann atá i lár na siúlóidí ar a bhfuil cur síos sa leabhar seo ainmnithe i ndiaidh an dea-dhuine sin Naomh Pádraig. Nach maith an ceart dom an t-eolas seo a thabhairt sa teanga seo?

MARTINDALE

Distance	4½ miles
Total Feet of Ascent	400 feet
Suggested Time	2 hours
Starting Point	St Martins Old Church (NY 434 184) Parking space in front of church *or Howtown Pier (NY 153 198)*

To some extent Martindale is cut off from the rest of the Lake District, most motorists seem to deem it too much out of the way to bother with. This then has the pleasing effect of making Martindale a relatively quiet valley, and yet once there it is unlikely you will be able to conceive of there being a more appealing dale anywhere else. Martindale, the name of which apparently derives from an ancient cross dedicated to St Martin which once stood in the valley, is actually not one single valley but two, Boardale and Bannerdale, or three if you include Rampsgill. They are so close to each other however, and each seems so like an extension of the other, it is hard not to think of them as one single valley. Dispersed throughout Martindale is a suprising variety of buildings and dwellings that evoke a strong sense of a vanished past.

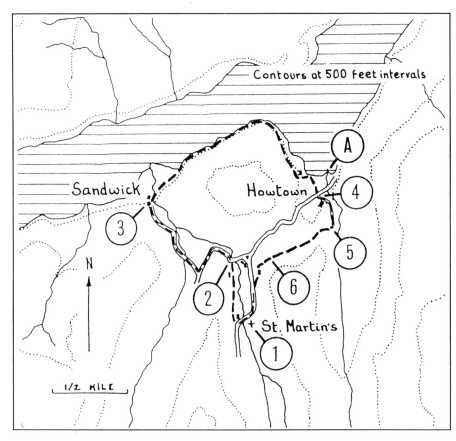

A *(If begining the walk from Howtown Pier walk directly from the pier to the roadway and turn right. A few hundred yards along the roadway turn first left, and from here follow note 4 onwards.)*

1 From the church follow the road south across a stone bridge. A hundred yards or so after crossing the bridge on your right is the start of a bridleway leading behind Winter Crag farm. After passing a very attractive little cottage the bridleway comes to a surfaced road. (½ mile)

2 Here turn left and follow the road. Where it comes to a junction turn right and follow the road to Sandwick. (1 mile)

3 At the end of the road a trackway continues to the right over a broad wooden bridge. This leads without difficulty round the base of Hallin Fell along the shoreline of Ullswater back to Howtown bay. A hundred yards after passing behind a large cream coloured house, Waternook, the path comes to a kissing gate. Here turn left through the kissing gate and down a flight of steps on to the trackway leading to Waternook. Turn right on the trackway and follow it to the Martindale road. (1¾ miles) *(If returning back to the Howtown pier here turn left, otherwise...)*

4 Immediately across the road is what appears to be a surfaced driveway to the Howtown Hotel. The road however leads behind the hotel and where it splits you should take the right hand branch to Cote Farm as far as the first cattle grid. (¼ mile)

5 Here turn right and follow the stone wall to your right uphill. This soon becomes a very evident grassy trackway, a bridleway, leading over Hallin Hause. Where however this bridleway begins to dip down and turn right, where there is a water hydrant marker, continue walking straight ahead along a very indistinct path following the left hand side of the wall ahead. The path soon comes to a small six bar gate. (½ mile)

6 Passing through the gate the path leads to two attractive cottages called Cotehow. Below them you should observe the valley's old methodist church and beside it an old reading room. Both are now domiciles. The building opposite them is the valley's former school. The right of way leads right through the front yard of Cotehow cottages and down to the roadway, though it is possible to skirt round the wall of the yard if you feel you are intruding too much on their privacy. On reaching the road turn left and follow the road back to St Martin's church. (½ mile)

PATTERDALE

Distance   6 ½ miles
Total Feet of Ascent   Negligible
Suggested Time   2½ hours
Starting Point   Patterdale Village car park (NY 396 159)

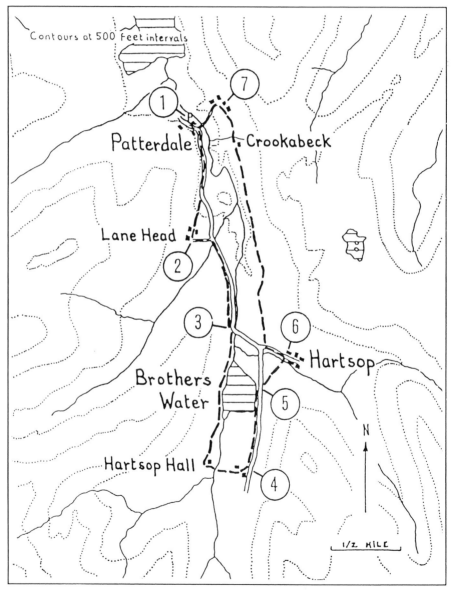

The Lake District is not particularly well designed for level walks. In the Patterdale area the only true level walk possible is the one described here, an elongated circuit of the valley floor itself. Unfortunately nearly half of the walk is along the side of, or little distance from, the A592, the main road which runs through the valley, which obviously detracts from the walk's tranquillity, though suprisingly not to the extent one might think. The final two miles of the walk however are decidedly more rural in quality and overall the walk affords the walker a good appreciation of the valley.

1 From the car park turn left and follow the road south. Roughly three quarters of a mile from Patterdale Post Office a driveway veers off to the right across a cattle grid signposted as being a public footpath to Deepdale leading initially to a little hamlet called Lane Head. (1 mile)

2 At Lane Head the driveway splits in two. Follow the left hand branch which turns left and leads back to the road. On reaching the road turn right. There is now no surfaced path along the side of the road, but along the right hand side of the road is a wide grass verge across which has worn a footpath. Follow this path. Within a quarter of a mile, starting from a single birch tree, the path rises above the level of the road and leads onto a permitted path that follows the road at a slightly higher level, through National Trust land, eventually reaching the start of a trackway leading from a sharp bend in an old section of the main road. (1 mile)

3 Here turn right and follow the trackway south past the western shoreline of Brotherswater. Eventually the path comes to curve left round Hartsop Hall where it branches in two. Follow the left hand branch which soon curves right and leads across a large campsite. Leaving the campsite the trackway branches in two once more. Follow the left hand branch. Five yards before it reaches the road leading off to the left is the start of a permitted path to Brotherswater. (1 ¼ miles)

4 Follow the permitted path which parallels the main road northwards mostly at a slightly lower level. It joins the the road briefly and then drops down to follow the eastern shoreline of Brotherswater. (In wet weather this path is prone to flooding). After passing through a kissing gate the path then leads up to a second kissing gate set in the wall bordering the road.(½ mile)

5 Directly across the road is a five bar gate. Cross over the road and pass through the gate. This leads on to an enclosed trackway that leads to a narrow footbridge crossing Pasture Beck giving access to the small village of Hartsop. (¼ mile)

6 On reaching the road running through the village turn left. (Though before you do so it is worth turning right to see what is one of the most appealing villages in the Lake District). Just before reaching the main road, to your right, leading north by the side of the Langton Adventure Centre, is a surfaced driveway. Continue along this driveway but where it curves right into 'Hartsop Fold' continue straight ahead along the unsurfaced trackway ahead of you. This is a delightful rustic trackway back to Patterdale village, though where it passes by an attractive dwelling called Crookabeck it may seem as if there is no longer a right of way along it, and indeed a permitted path is indicated as running behind the house; however a right of way does continue along the trackway. Within a short distance from Crookabeck it reaches a small hamlet. (2 miles)

7 Here the track joins a surfaced driveway. Turn left and follow the driveway back to the start of the walk. (¼ mile)

GRISEDALE

Distance	7 miles
Total Feet of Ascent	700 feet
Suggested Time	3 hours
Starting Point	Patterdale village car park (NY 396 159)

Though not perfectly level this walk should be well within the range of even the most unenergetic of walkers, yet from it can be appreciated some of the wildest mountain terrain in the Lake District. Grisedale is an impressive valley. It is the largest valley of those valleys in the Lake District which do not have a surfaced road, apart from Ennerdale. The head of the valley is overlooked by some huge imposing crags. All this is possible to view and appreciate with relatively little effort, yet a few miles away in the village of Patterdale one is hardly aware of such magnificence existing at all.

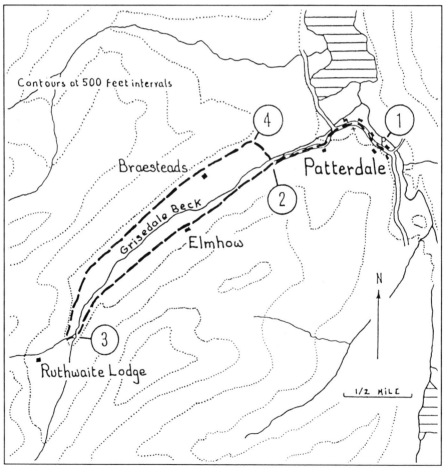

1 From Patterdale car park walk northwards along the road 700 yards past the church and take the first turn left on to an unsignposted surfaced road. This road soon splits in two. Take the right branch which soon curves right climbing uphill a hundred feet or so before levelling out. After a short distance of level walking an uninterrupted view of Grisdedale is obtained shortly after which a trackway, signposted for Helvellyn, veers off to the right. (1 mile)

2 Ignore this trackway and continue progressing forward on the surfaced roadway. After a short distance the road splits in two with the right hand branch crossing over a stone bridge and leading to Braesteads Farm. Ignore this branch and continue walking straight ahead. The road soon becomes roughly surfaced trackway. Passing Elmhow Farm it becomes rougher still and beyond an isolated barn, a couple of hundred yards further on from Elmhow, it reduces to a bridleway, which after a few hundred feet of climbing eventually comes to a wooden footbridge crossing over Grisedale Beck. (2¼ miles)

3 Crossing over the footbridge the bridleway continues climbing uphill roughly parallel to a tributary of Grisedale Beck flowing from Ruthwaite Cove. About two hundred yards from the Grisedale Beck footbridge is a second footbridge crossing over this tributary. Cross over this second footbridge and follow the path that leads from it back down Grisedale on the northern side of the valley. Eventually, just before reaching a wooden kissing gate, the path is crossed by a path leading down from Striding Edge. (2½ miles)

4 Here turn right and follow the Striding Edge path, through a small gate in the wall to your right, downhill through another kissing gate onto a trackway that leads over a stone bridge and back to the road which you began on. Here turn left and retrace your route back to Patterdale. (1¼ miles)

THE ULLSWATER LAKESHORE PATH

Distance	7 miles
Total Feet of Ascent	Between 500 and 1000 feet.
Suggested Time	3 hours, excluding time travelling on lake.
Starting Point	Patterdale village car park. (NY 396 159).
Public Transport	Ullswater motoryacht. Glenridding to Howtown. Seasonal only, Easter to October. Operators Ullswater Navigation Company Tel. 07684 82229

This is one of the most popular lakeshore walks in the Lake District. Part of its appeal no doubt lies in the fact that it also involves taking a short boat trip on Ullswater. I have here described the complete lakeshore path, but the walk can be varied, and in my own view bettered, by first diverting into Martindale to begin with. This you can do by following the route from Howtown to Sandwick described in the Martindale walk on page 6. This would add about an extra mile to the walk and a few hundred feet of extra climbing.

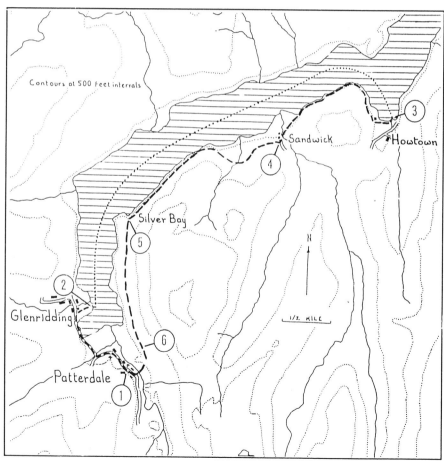

1 Leaving the car park turn right and follow the road to Glenridding. There is a footpath along the side of the road on either one side or the other until the road comes to parallel the lake. Here a path runs a little above the road through the trees on the lefthand side of the road. On reaching Glenridding follow the well indicated trackway leading to Glenridding pier. (1 mile)

2 From the pier use one of the two Ullswater motoryachts to sail to Howtown.

3 After walking a few yards from the Howtown pier turn right over a wooden footbridge and follow the lake shore path. This soon joins a trackway where you should turn right. Follow the trackway a hundred yards and then turn off to the left, through a kissing gate, on to a signposted path to Patterdale and Sandwick. This climbs up to another kissing gate passing through which you come onto a broad pathway traversing around the lower slopes of Hallin Fell. Here turn right. This path is so distinctive there is no problem in following it around Hallin Fell to Sandwick, a small hamlet situated in a little area of farmland on the shoreline of the lake squeezed between Hallin Fell and Place Fell. Here the path joins the termination of the surfaced road which leads to to the hamlet. (1¾ miles)

4 Turn left and follow the road fifty yards to the start of a signposted path veering off to the right past the side of Townhead Cottage. This is the continuation of the shore line path which traverses the lower slopes of Place Fell. This is one of the steepest and rockiest fellsides in the Lake District but the path makes such an easy job of traversing along it you may be hardly aware of these qualities, but because of them the path itself rises and falls a good deal - and this you will be aware of. Coming to a small bay, Silver Bay, the path curves round to the right, and just before reaching the corner of this curve, the start of it marked with a suprisingly large cairn, a path veers uphill to the left. (2 miles)

5 Here turn left to take the higher path which has better views than the lower path as further on it passes behind a band of trees and a high stone wall before coming to Patterdale. Eventually the higher path reaches a small cave-like quarry. (1½ miles)

6 Just after passing the quarry the path makes a sharp hairpin bend, but from the corner of this bend what would seem to be the original course of the path continues forward, through some more old quarry workings and then dips down. Where it begins to rise a trackway branches down to the right to a five bar gate. Passing through this gate you come onto a surfaced driveway. Here turn left. The driveway soon curves round to the right to join the main valley road a few hundred yards south of the car park where the walk began. (½ mile)

THE GOWBARROW CIRCUIT

Distance	8 miles
Total Feet of Ascent	1200 feet
Suggested Time	4 hours
Starting Point	Aira Force Car Park (NY 400 200).

This is quite a varied walk. To begin with it follows the side of Aira Force, the most accessible waterfall in the Lake District, which is the problem for at the wrong time of day the area around the falls is inundated with visitors. Leaving it behind however you soon enter a far more peaceful area, with narrow winding lanes, that reflect very strongly a quieter rural past. The final three miles or so are along a fairly easy open fellside path, from the final mile of which is obtained some of the best views of Ullswater and Patterdale possible.

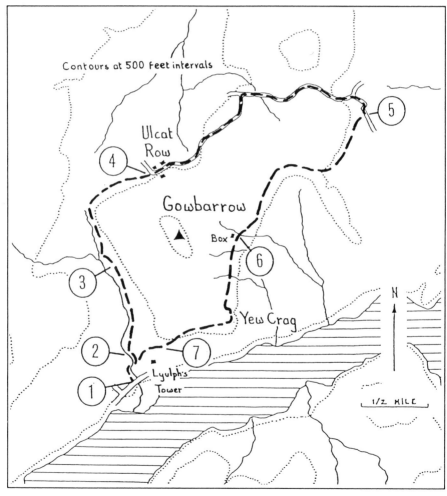

1 Follow the broad path leading from the far end of the car park. Where this diverges in two take the broader right hand branch which crosses over a footbridge and begins climbing uphill. This again soon branches in two. This time take the left hand branch. After a few hundred yards the path branches in two again, the right hand branch zig-zagging up a flight of steps. It is the right hand branch you should follow, though before you do so you will doubtless wish to follow the left hand branch a few yards to a stone bridge from which position you can view the falls. (½ mile)

2 The right hand path climbs up to a second bridge spanning the top of the falls. Apart from using it to admire the the falls do not cross it but keep to the path following the eastern side of the beck. This soon diverges in two. Follow the right hand branch which is stepped and leads to a kissing gate through which it joins a broader path which continues to follow the beck northwards. This too soon divides in two with the left hand branch leading down to a footbridge crossing the beck. Ignore this however and continue along the right hand branch which emerging from the woods enclosing the beck soon reaches a six bar gate with a smaller wicket gate beside it. (¾ mile)

3 Passing through the gate and across a small beck the path becomes more of a trackway. A hundred yards or so further on, just before reaching an isolated dwelling place, another trackway branches off to the right signposted as leading to Ulcat Row. Continue along this trackway, which follows the side of a long wall to the small hamlet of Ulcat Row where it joins a roadway. (1 mile)

4 Here turn right and follow the road to its junction with a second road and here turn right again. After descending some four hundred feet, and some three hundred yards past the entrance to a caravan site, to your right, through a kissing gate, is the start of a signed path to Aira Force. (2 miles)

5 There is no difficulty in following this path, though after initially starting off as a very broad path it does become quite narrow. It takes quite an unusual line traversing along the eastern and southern slopes of Gowbarrow Fell, to a small stone ruin, marked variously as a Shooting Lodge or Shooting Box on the OS maps. (1¾ miles)

6 From this ruin the path rises a little further up to a wooden footbridge spanning the top of a steep gully after which the path keeps a roughly level course for half a mile and then branches in two. Continue along the left hand lower branch, which in moving around the promontory of Yew Crag provides some wonderful views of Ullswater and Patterdale. After a steep descent the path draws level with Lyulph's Tower and merges with another path. (1½ miles)

7 A hundred yards or so beyond this merger point just as the path begins to climb uphill again a grassier path veers off to the left towards a simple wooden stile. Crossing over this stile the path joins a much broader path. Here turn left. The path soon merges with the path you began on leading from the car park. (½ mile)

GOWBARROW TOP

Distance	4½ miles
Total Feet of Ascent	1200 feet
Suggested Time	3 hours
Starting Point	Aira Force Car Park (NY 400 200).

This walk is a shorter version of the walk described on the previous two pages, the main difference being, of course, that this walk crosses over the summit of Gowbarrow. Much of the previous walk's description therefore also applies here. Gowbarrow is a very wide rambling fell so the actual summit is not very distinct though the views from it are well worth seeing. It is along the shoreline of Ullswater beneath Gowbarrow that William and Dorothy Wordsworth saw growing the daffodils which inspired the writing of the best known poem in the English lanquage. Though what is specifically lonely about a cloud I do not know. From my own observations I would say the average cloud in the Lake District on the whole enjoys far too much company.

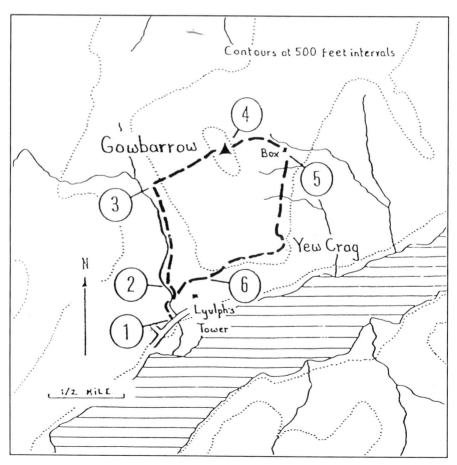

1 Follow the broad path leading from the far end of the car park. Where this diverges in two take the broader right hand branch which crosses over a footbridge and begins climbing uphill. This again soon branches in two. This time take the left hand branch. After a few hundred yards the path branches in two again, the right hand branch zig-zagging up a flight of steps. It is the right hand branch you should follow, though before you do so you will doubtless wish to follow the left hand branch a few yards to a stone bridge from which position you can view the falls. (½ mile)

2 The right hand path climbs up to a second bridge spanning the top of the falls. Apart from using it to admire the the falls do not cross it but keep to the path following the eastern side of the beck. This soon diverges in two. Follow the right hand branch which is stepped and leads to a kissing gate through which it joins a broader path which continues to follow the beck northwards. This too soon divides in two with the left hand branch leading down to a footbridge crossing the beck. Ignore this however and continue along the right hand branch which emerging from the woods enclosing the beck soon reaches a six bar gate with a smaller wicket gate beside it. (¾ mile)

3 Here turn right and follow a very indistinct path following the side of the wall leading uphill from the gate past the side of a small copse of conifer trees. (There is a sign pointing to this path but unless it has been repaired by the time this guide is printed it is likely to have fallen down!). Crossing over a stone stile the path becomes more distinctive. On drawing level with the wall's highest point the path divides in two. Follow the right hand branch which leads to the summit of Gowbarrow a few hundred yards away marked with a trig point. (¾ mile)

4 From the trig point follow the path leading north-eastwards along the crest of the little heather clad ridge the trig point is situated on. The path continues to follow, though not so closely, the same wall you followed to the top of Gowbarrow as it descends down the other side of the fell eventually reaching a small stone ruin, marked variously as a Shooting Lodge or a Shooting Box on the OS maps where it joins another path. (½ mile)

5 Here turn right and follow the new path as it climbs a little uphill to a wooden footbridge spanning the top of a steep gully, after which it keeps a roughly level course for half a mile and then branches in two. Continue along the left hand lower branch, which in moving around the promontory of Yew Crag provides some splendid views of Ullswater and Patterdale. After a steep descent the path draws level with Lyulph's Tower and merges with another path. (1½ miles)

6 A hundred yards or so beyond this merger point just as the path begins to climb uphill again a grassier path veers off to the left towards a simple wooden stile. Crossing over this stile the path joins a much broader path. Here turn left. The path soon merges with the path you began on leading from the car park. (½ mile)

SHEFFIELD PIKE 2215 feet

Distance	5 ½ miles
Total Feet of Ascent	1800 feet
Suggested Time	4 hours
Starting Point	Glenridding Car Park (NY 386 170).

There are some impressive views from this fell, as being a slightly lower felltop it has several higher fells around it to admire. However, despite the very considerable and impressive efforts made to remove and landscape the industrial scars left behind by the lead mining activities which once took place in the Glenridding valley, it has to be admitted that ascending through these remains to the top of Sheffield Pike is still a fairly unglamorous experience. However the descent route does much to compensate. An even better descent route yet is to follow the last three and a half miles of the Dodds walk described on page 30. This would take you to Dockray from whence you could follow the path by Aira Force down to the lakeshore of Ullswater from which point it would be possible to bus back to Glenridding.

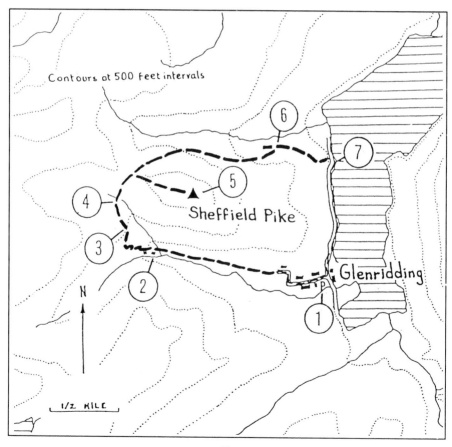

1 From the Information Office follow the exit sign out of the car park but turn immediately left at the electricity substation and then immediately right by the side of a grey wooden shed onto a surfaced pathway signposted as leading to Helvellyn which initially leads to Greenside Road. Here turn left and follow the road uphill. After passing the Travellers Rest it soon splits in two. Continue along the right hand branch which to begin with is surfaced but after curving left soon becomes a rough surfaced trackway leading to the Helvellyn Youth Hostel. (1¼ miles)

2 Just past the youth hostel is the Bury Jubilee Outdoor Pursuits Centre after which the trackway divides in two. The right hand branch is well signed as leading to Sticks Pass and continues to be well signposted and waymarked as it becomes a rough surfaced pathway zig-zagging its way up through the old industrial wastes of Greenside mine until you reach a sign headed 'Greenside Mine Area', meant for people descending the path, where the waymarking ends. (½ mile)

3 Here the path actually diverges in two. One branch continues straight on ahead whilst the path to Sticks Pass veers uphill to the left. Continue along the path to Sticks Pass which after a short rocky climb reaches some wooden sleepers. It may again seem at this point as if the path has turned sharp left. The line of rubble leading uphill to your left however is the remains of a flue which took away the poisonous fumes of the mine's lead smelting activity. Do not mistake it for the Sticks Pass path which continues leading straight ahead and soon becomes fairly grassy. Where the path levels to be almost flat begin looking for a very imprecise path leading off to the right immediately after crossing a very boggy section of the path. (¼ mile)

4 This thin grassy path crosses Sticks Gill and leads to the top of the gap between Green Side and Sheffield Pike which is marked with a small pile of white stones. As you near the gap you will find the path gets more defined but near the beck especially the line of the path is almost impossible to discover. Should the beck be in spate there is a footbridge a little up stream where the Stick's path crosses it. Arriving at the small cairn of white stones marking the top of the gap between Green Side and Sheffield Pike turn right and follow a thin grassy path leading to the top of the Pike. The views from the top of Sheffield Pike are extremely good especially of Ullswater which are better still if you walk a few yards north-eastwards towards the lake. (¾ mile)

5 From the summit return back to the small cairn of white stones at the top of the saddle between the Pike and Green Side and turn right. The delicate path leading to the right from the cairn makes a gradual descent into Glencoyne and eventually comes to follow the side of a solid stone wall. Keep to the right hand side of the wall and ignore a path which a few hundred yards along the wall passes through it and leads directly towards the cottages at Seldom Seen. The path following the outer side of the wall eventually joins a rough unsurfaced access road leading to the Seldom Seen cottages. (1½ miles)

6 Here turn right and follow the access road down to the main road. (½ mile)

7 On the other side of the road, behind the small wall bordering it, is a pathway which parallels the road. Turn right and follow the path towards Glenridding. This is a constructed path and seems as if it once may have been the main route into the valley. Nearing Stybarrow Crag the path merges with the road but soon veers off to the left again. After leaving the road be careful to take a flight of steps you come to shortly afterwards. Finally the path rejoins the road again just before arriving back at Glenridding. (1 mile)

PLACE FELL 2154 feet

Distance   8 ½ miles
Total Feet of Ascent   Between 2000 and 2500 feet
Suggested Time   5 ½ hours
Starting Point   Patterdale Village car park (NY 396 159)

This is an appealing fell that is none too difficult to ascend. The descent also gives some appreciation of Martindale arriving as it does at Sandwick Farm, a small lakeside hamlet squeezed in bewteen Place Fell and Hallin Fell. From here the route returns back to Patterdale along the popular eastern shoreline path of Ullswater, thus giving the walk a great variety of interest and contrasts.

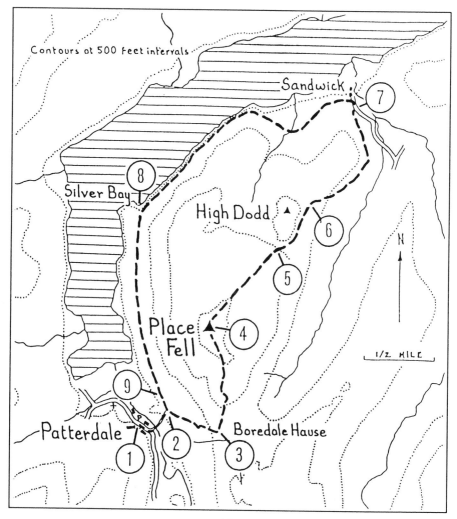

1 From the car park turn left and walk south along the main road a few few hundred yards and take the first turn left. After about a hundred yards the road forks. Take the left branch. Within a hundred yards this branches in to three trackways. Take the middle track signposted to Boredale Hause. This soon reduces to a pathway and pulls sharply uphill within a few yards to another pathway. (½ mile)

2 Here turn right. After a few hundred yards this path splits in two. Follow the left hand, higher, branch which is the original packhorse route crossing over Boredale Hause. After a climb of a few hundred feet, near to an isolated hawthorn bush, the path zig zags back on itself. Be careful to follow this zig-zag otherwise it is easy to follow by mistake a path branching off the packhorse path and linking on to the lower parallel path. Keeping to the original packhorse path about a hundred yards from the crest of the pass you should arrive at a very dilapidated sheepfold. (½ mile)

3 At this point another path crosses over the packhorse path. Here turn left and follow the new path uphill. It leads without difficulty to the top of Place Fell, the summit of which is marked with a trig point. The best views from the top however are obtained by walking a few yards westwards from the trig point to a position where you can look down on Ullswater and Glenridding and across the valley to Helvellyn. (1 mile)

4 From the trig point the path continues to Martindale passing the left hand side of a summit tarn. It then makes a gentle descent to the saddle between Place Fell itself and High Dodd where there is situated a ruined sheepfold. (¾ mile)

5 From the sheepfold the path splits in two, with the left hand branch curving leftwards and descending directly down to Sandwick, whilst the right hand branch continues directly ahead rising uphill slightly. Continue along the right hand branch which soon begins descending. Within half a mile the path branches in two again with the right hand branch making a sharp descent down hill. (½ mile)

6 Continue along the right hand branch. Nearing the bottom of the valley the path comes to follow a stone wall northwards curving round the side of the valley and climbing slightly as the valley deepens. Where the wall makes a sharp turn right continue following the path straight ahead down to the roadway running below you. (1 mile)

7 On reaching the road turn left. A hundred yards along the road veering off to the left is a signposted path to Patterdale. This soon becomes a broad stony path following a solid stone wall which goes on to traverse the lower slopes of Place Fell. This is one of the steepest and rockiest fellsides in the Lake District but the path makes such an easy job of traversing along it you may be hardly aware of these qualities, but because of them the path itself rises and falls a good deal - and this you will be aware of. Coming to a small bay, Silver Bay, the path curves round to the right, and just before reaching the corner of this curve, the start of it marked with a suprisingly large cairn, a path veers uphill to the left. (2¼ miles)

8 Here turn left to take the higher path which has better views than the lower path, as further on it passes behind a band of trees and a high stone wall before coming to Patterdale. Eventually the higher path reaches a small cave-like quarry. (1½ miles)

9 Just after passing the quarry the path makes a sharp hairpin bend, but from the corner of this bend what would seem to be the original course of the path continues forward through some more old quarry workings and then dips down. Where it begins to rise a trackway branches down to the right to a five bar gate, which you will doubtless recognise as the gate you passed at the start of the walk. Pass back through the gate and retrace your earlier route back to the car park. (½ mile)

DOVE CRAG 2603 feet

Distance	8 miles
Total Feet of Ascent	2100 feet
Suggested Time	5 hours
Starting Point	Brotherswater car park (NY 402 133).

This walk takes in two attractive and little known valleys; Dovedale and Caiston Glen. Dovedale is especially attractive; a tight, twisting little valley with a very complex shape. Caiston is suprisingly peaceful even though in its lower parts the busy A592 is less than a quarter mile away. The object of the walk, Dove Crag, is part of the popular Fairfield Horseshoe so you are likely to meet a fair number of walkers once you get on to it. These numbers quickly dwindle again once you turn towards Scandale Pass, to such an extent that you may feel there is no one on the hill but yourself.

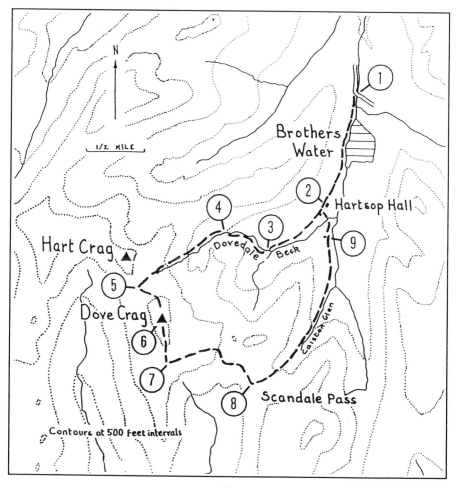

1 From the car park pass through a five bar gate on to a trackway running along side of Brotherswater to Hartsop Hall. (1 mile)

2 At Hartsop Hall the trackway curves round the farm and comes to a T-junction with another trackway. Here turn right and follow the track past the right hand side of some outbuildings. After passing these buildings a path branches off to the right signposted as a 'permitted path'. Ignore this path and keep to the trackway signposted as a 'public footpath'. Keep to your side of Dovedale Beck, eventually walking across a smooth sward to a footbridge screened by a holly bush. (¾ mile)

3 Cross the footbridge over Dovedale Beck and turn right, following a distinct uphill path. This soon crosses over a tributary of Dovedale Beck and then follows the side of Dovedale Beck itself. In one or two places the path has a tendency to branch in two and then merge back again. To avoid any confusion choose the option closest to the beck itself. This will eventually bring you to a wooden stile constructed over a former gate. (½ mile)

4 Having crossed the stile you should cross straight over Dovedale Beck and climb fifty feet or so up to a very obvious pathway on the other side. Here turn left and follow the path uphill. This is a distinctive path, if somewhat steep at times, leading to the col between Dove Crag and Hart Crag. (1 mile)

5 Here turn left and follow the ridge, along the side of a dilapidated wall, on to the top of Dove Crag. (¼ mile)

6 From the summit of Dove Crag continue following the ruined wall crossing over the summit southwards towards Ambleside. A few hundred yards from the summit the remains of a metal fence leads away to the left from the wall. After this point in the space of the next couple of hundred yards you should discover two cairns sited to the left of the wall. From the second, the furthest of these two cairns, a grassy pathway leads off to the left. (½ mile)

7 Follow this pathway. It soon reaches a strange group of cairns after which it becomes fairly indistinct. However, continue advancing downhill in the same direction in which you arrived at the cairns and within a short distance you should have no problem making out the path again as it leads down to the top of Scandale Pass. (1 mile)

8 Here turn left and follow the path downhill into Caiston Glen towards the head of Patterdale. Eventually the path leads to an isolated barn. (1¾ miles)

9 Passing through the barn's adjacent yard the path becomes a trackway which leads back to Hartsop Hall from where you can follow your earlier route back to the walk's starting point. (1¼ miles)

THORNTHWAITE CRAG 2569 feet

Distance	6 ½ miles
Total Feet of Ascent	2700
Suggested Time	5 hours
Starting Point	Hartsop car park. (NY 410 131)

This walk involves using two ridges that run either side of the Pasture Beck valley. They are both fairly slender, the second one between Thornthwaite Crag and Grey Crag particularly so, and afford the walker a great sense of elevation and fine views of the surrounding, slightly higher, fells. The starting ascent up Hartsop Dodd is very steep and demanding however, whilst the gap between the two ridges is also suprisingly rugged. For these reasons the walk is probably not the best walk for a novice fellwalker to begin on.

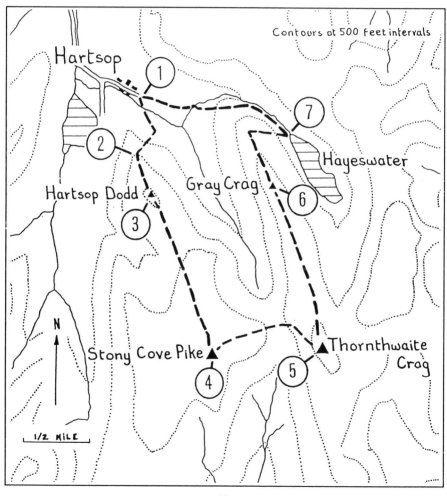

1 From the kissing gate exiting from the car park at the end of Hartsop village bear right along the track signposted for Pasture Beck. After crossing over the beck where the track makes a sharp turn left follow the wall to your right directly uphill. In the corner of the field just to the right of a line of fir trees is a wooden stile. From here the path continues to follow the right hand wall to the crest of the steep ridge leading up to Hartsop Dodd. (¼ mile)

2 On reaching the crest of the ridge turn left and follow it to the top of Hartsop Dodd. The ridge has a convexed slope towards the top so it has a number of illusory 'summits' including one with a distinct cairn which turns out to be the end elevation of a stone wall; after reaching this though the true summit is only a short distance away. (½ mile)

3 From the top of Hartsop Dodd the path continues along this wall which follows the crest of the ridge leading from Hartsop Dodd to Stony Cove Pike. The top of Stony Cove Pike is one of the flattest tops in the Lake District. Its actual highest point is hard to determine. There are two distinct cairns both some fifty yards distance away from either side of the wall's highest point. The cairn to the right definitely does not mark the summit. The cairn to the left, however, possibly does. For the purpose of these direction notes we shall assume it is the summit. (1¼ miles)

4 From the summit cairn a path curves away in an easterly direction. Within a few yards it comes to follow the line of a dilapidated wall leading down to Threshthwaite Mouth, a deep pass between Stony Cove Pike and Thornthwaite Crag. The final part of this descent is particularly rugged and rocky. On reaching the pass continue to follow the wall as it climbs steeply uphill from the pass to the summit of Thornthwaite Crag, the top of which is surmounted with a beacon, a tall slender cairn, that from a distance looks like a chimney. (1 mile)

5 From the beacon, moving in a north to north-westerly direction, follow the slightly undulating crest of the long slender ridge running from Thornthwaite Crag to Gray Crag. (1¼ miles)

6 From the top of Gray Crag the ridge becomes quite narrow and steep. There is however a distinct break in the steepness of this gradient after passing a trench-like feature centred along the ridge's crest, after which the ridge steepens again. At this point it is best to abandon following the ridge and instead head directly for the outflow of Hayeswater. There is no path but the ground is easy enough to descend across and the gradient is much easier than it would be if you were to stick to the ridge. (¾ mile)

7 From Hayeswater a broad distinct trackway leads directly back to Hartsop village. (1¼ miles)

HIGH STREET 2719 feet

Distance	9 miles
Total Feet of Ascent	2400 feet
Suggested Time	5 ½ hours
Starting Point	Hartsop car park.(NY 410 131).

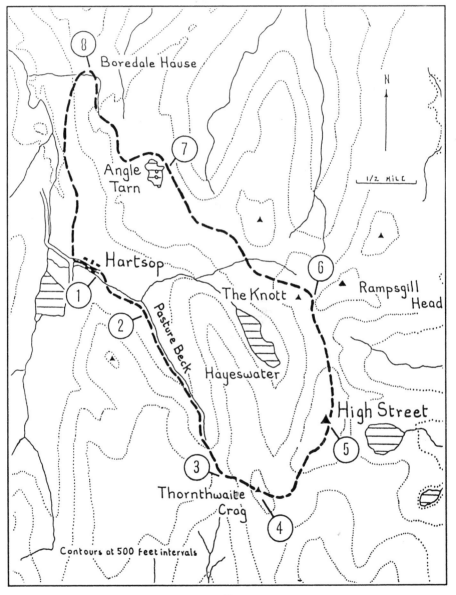

High Street acquires its name from the fact that a Roman Road once crossed over its summit. It is a very broad and flat top and because of these qualities it was once possible for it to have been used as a site for a race course. If you look closely at the O.S. 1:25,000 map you can see that High Street is also called Racecourse Hill. This goes back to the days of the Mardale Shepherd Meet, when once a year the shepherds of Mardale, the valley now submerged under Haweswater Reservoir, met other shepherds from the neighbouring valleys on the top of High Street to exchange back the sheep which had strayed from their own valleys into their neighbours', and as part of the day's events they also held horse races on this lofty fell top. But like the Roman Road there is now little evidence, if any, of this former course left to be seen.

1 Exit Hartsop car park through the kissing gate at its eastern edge and immediately turn right down to a bridge and continue on the distinct path ahead of you to a five bar gate. Pass through the gate and turn left. Follow the path along the wall into Pasture Beck valley. (½ mile)

2 The path along the valley is lightly used compared with other Lakeland paths but is easy enough to follow. A final steep climb at the head of the valley brings you to Threshthwaite Mouth, the col between Stony Cove Pike and Thornthwaite Crag. (1¼ miles)

3 From the col tackle the steep climb up to your left along the side of a dilapidated wall to the summit of Thornthwaite Crag which is topped by the tallest summit cairn in the Lake District, which from a distance has the appearance of a chimney stack. (¼ mile)

4 From Thornthwaite Crag a very obvious path curves north-eastwards round the head of the Hayeswater valley onto the summit of High Street involving a climb of less than 200 feet. The precise summit is marked by a large white trig point set in the middle of the stone wall following the crest of the fell. (1 mile)

5 From the summit of High Street follow the stone wall northwards. After ¾ mile a path veers off to the right towards Rampsgill Head. Ignore this path and continue following the wall to the shallow gap between Rampsgill Head and the Knott. (1 mile)

6 The path moves round The Knott and begins to descend in a north-westerly direction. After about 300 feet of descent the path splits in two, though you may hardly notice this as the right hand branch which you should follow is much bolder than the left hand branch that continues straight ahead down to Hayeswater. Continue following the bolder right hand path which after a few more feet of descent and crossing a distinct beck called Sulphry Gill then traverses the lower slopes of Rest Dodd and crosses Satura Crag to arrive at Angle Tarn. (1¾ miles)

7 The path continues around the northern edge of Angle Tarn and leads to Boredale Hause, the gap between Place Fell and the Angle Tarn Pikes. (1 mile)

8 From Boredale Hause the path continues down to Patterdale village. Follow this path a short way to a point where suprisingly a cast iron pipe emerges out of the ground emitting a refreshing trickle of water. At this point a less distinct path veers off to the left. Follow this path down to the foot of the fell where it joins a trackway leading south back to Hartsop village and the start of the walk. (1¾ miles)

HIGH RAISE 2634 feet

Distance	10 miles
Total Feet of Ascent	2200 feet
Suggested Time	6 hours
Starting Point	St Martin's Old Church, Martindale (NY 434 184)
	Parking space in front of church.

This is a very quiet walk except where it follows Wainwright's Coast to Coast path, between Rampsgill Head and Angle Tarn, where you are likely to see a good many walkers. The highest part of the walk, between Red Crag and Rampsgill Head, a broad peat covered ridge, though pleasant, is fairly unspectacular. The ascent to it on the other hand is quite stimulating. Probably the most attractive point of the walk is Angle Tarn. With its open uncrowded setting it is probably the most attractive tarn in the Lake District.

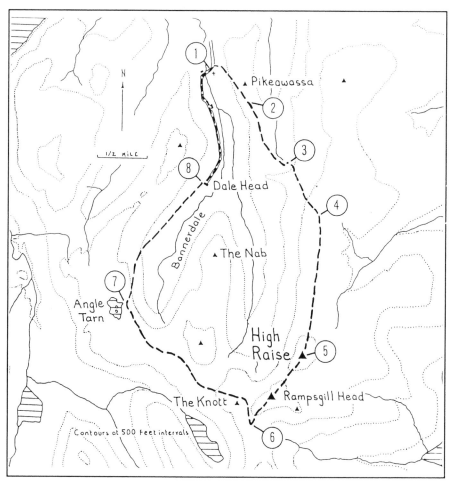

1   From St Martin's church walk northwards along the road about a hundred yards and stand by a metal gate to your left leading to an isolated barn. Look directly at the fellside across the road. Observe the largest rock in front of you about a hundred foot above the road; running just past the left hand side of the rock is a very imperceptible pathway, a more perceptible path can be seen a few yards more to the left, and a very distinct track leads to the right behind the church, but it is the path that touches the left hand side of the rock itself you should follow. I suspect this is not the original start of the path, which has long since been overgrown with ferns, for after following it uphill a few hundred feet it becomes a lot more distinctive and was obviously very carefully constructed in the past taking a diagonal line up the fell to reach the crest of the ridge just to the south of the splendidly named little peak of Pikeawassa. (¾ mile)

2   The path follows the line of the ridge southwards and where there might be any doubt as to the line of the path veer towards the wall running along the crest of the ridge. Within a short distance the ridge broadens and the path descends a little and veers off to the left traversing round the head of the short valley of Fusedale to an isolated ruined stone barn. (¾ mile)

3   From the gable end of the barn a thin grassy path leads uphill soon veering to the right and becoming more distinct. Within a short distance it is evident that this too was a constructed path and may well be a continuation of the path you began on. Nearing the crest of the High Street range, which the path takes a diagonal course towards, the path curves around the head of a stony little gully and reaches two wooden gateposts the gate of which lies on the ground in a few disintegrated pieces. (¾ mile)

4   From here the path follows the line of the fence directly ahead on to the crest of the ridge where it parallels a ruined wall. Where the fence eventually comes to take a sharp turn right the path continues straight ahead towards High Raise though it actually passes to the right of the summit. (1½ miles)

5   From High Raise the path dips down a few hundred feet and then climbs up to Rampsgill Head. Crossing over which and descending a little way down the other side it comes to join a very broad worn path running along the side of a very long ruined wall. (1 mile)

6   Here turn right and follow the wall northwards. Where the wall takes a sharp left turn up to the top of a small hillock called The Knott the path continues straight ahead curving round The Knott and leading downhill. After about 300 feet of descent the path splits in two, though you may hardly notice this as the right hand branch which you should follow is much bolder than the left hand branch that continues straight ahead down to Hayeswater. Continue following the bolder right hand path which, after a few more feet of descent, traverses the lower slopes of Rest Dodd and crosses Satura Crag to arrive at Angle Tarn. (2 miles)

7   Immediately you draw level with the narrow stretch of water between the two little islands in Angle Tarn turn sharp right and cross over the low gap between the tarn and Bannerdale in a line towards the top of The Nab on the other side of Bannerdale if it is clear enough to see. Within a few yards you should see below you quite a solid wall running diagonally down the fellside into Bannerdale. A little to your left perhaps, if you are not already following it, you should locate a thin grassy path leading down to and then following the wall. Crossing an area of scree the path takes a higher course than the wall and becomes little wider than a sheep trod. It rejoins the wall futher down the valley and imperceptibly becomes a broad grassy trackway leading to Dale Head Farm. (1¾ miles)

8   From the farm a surfaced road leads back to St Martin's church. (1¼ miles)

THE DODDS

Distance	10 miles
Highest Point	Great Dodd 2807 feet.
Total Feet of Ascent	2200 feet
Suggested Time	6 hours
Starting Point	Dockray (NY 393 215)

This is mostly a very dull featureless walk, in mist it would be almost impossible to navigate round. Apart from it including what is technically one of the highest peaks in the area covered by this guide, which therefore might make it of interest to ardent 'peak baggers', it would have little to recommend it were it not also for the fact that the descent route involves taking a quite exceptional path that was developed by miners as a way of reaching their place of work from their homes in Dockray. From this path are to be obtained some of the finest views possible of Ullswater and the Patterdale valley, to quote Wainwright - "Here the keen camera enthusiast will suffer a paroxysm of enthusiasm". The benefits of this particular path can also be included in the Sheffield Pike walk described on page 18.

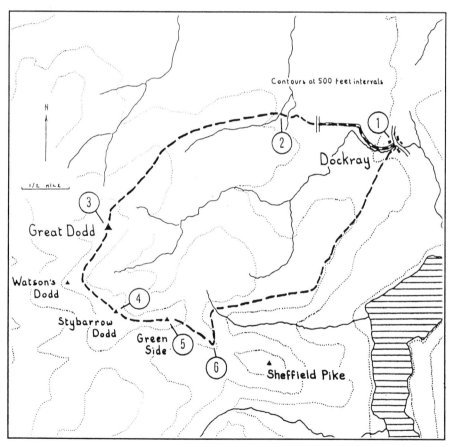

1 From Dockray follow the road signposted for Dowthwaite Head. Where the road comes to a crossroads continue straight ahead along a roughly surfaced road signposted as leading to Threlkeld and marked on the map as an old coach road. Twenty yards after the old coach road fords Groove Beck a rough trackway veers off to the left. (1½ miles)

2 Continue along this track which almost immediately acquires a grassy surface and soon has the qualities of a simple path. Reaching level terrain the ground becomes a quagmire and the line of the path is barely visible and would probably be completely impossible to follow in mist. As the gradient increases the path again becomes discernible and remains so until within a few hundred feet of the summit of Great Dodd when it disappears completely. Two widely spaced cairns however indicate a line of ascent to the summit cairn which even in mist should be easy enough to locate even though it seems to be a few yards from the actual highest point. (2½ miles)

3 From the summit cairn walk a few hundred yards south-east to a circular stone shelter. From here head in a southerly direction along the crest of the ridge towards Watson's Dodd. A distinct path soon develops which after a short descent becomes quite level and skirts past Watson's Dodd and then begins to climb uphill. Where this path starts to become level again, veering away from the crest of the ridge to contour round the side of it, strike directly uphill to your left. Within a hundred yards you should reach a cairn with a thick oblong slab of slate set upright in the middle which could well mark the true summit of Stybarrow Dodd. (1¼ miles)

4 From here walk due south-east. After a descent of about 200 feet you should be able to discern a path leading eastwards. This path rises to the top of Green Side, a broad hillock strewn with rocks and surmounted with a cairn. A hundred yards on is a second cairn and a hundred yards further on still is a third. (¾ mile)

5 From this third cairn head south east to Sheffield Pike. The descent soon becomes very steep and you should be able to locate a thin narrow grassy path. Beware though of a steep quarry just to the right of this descent which is not marked on the smaller scale Ordnance Survey maps. About 100 feet above the col between Green Side and Sheffield Pike, called Nick Head, a broad grassy path, distinguishable mostly by the different colour of its vegetation cover, cuts across your line of descent roughly following the contour of the fell. (½ mile)

6 Here turn left to follow this new path. It soon becomes quite narrow and takes a remarkable course around the head of Glencoynedale,and then along the northern side of the valley, nearly always keeping to the same contour. At the mouth of the valley it crosses a section of open fell and then follows the line of a wall for almost a mile from which some very impressive views of Ullswater and Patterdale are obtainable. Eventually the path veers to the left away from the wall and leads directly across a final quagmire back to Dockray.(3½ miles)

THE DEEPDALE HORSESHOE

Distance	9 miles
Highest Point	Fairfield 2863 feet
Total Feet of Ascent	3000 feet
Suggested Time	6 hours
Starting Point	Bridge End (NY 399 143). Small parking space next to the telephone box.

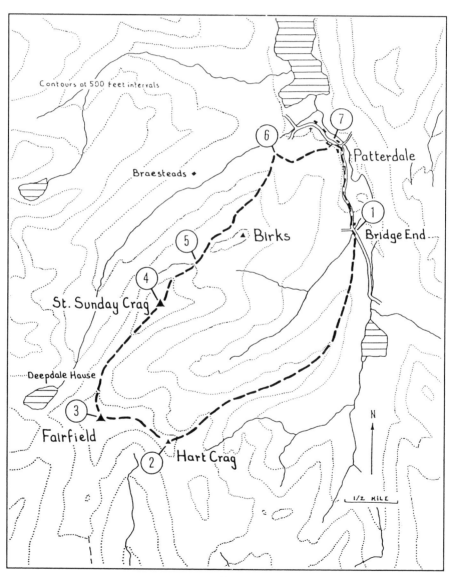

This is a very enjoyable and satisfying high level fell walk, with some quite dramatic sections. The ascent ridge to Hart Crag has excellent views of the fells which crowd round the head of Patterdale, including the impressive crags of Fairfield and the more rounded fells of Cauldale Moor to the east. Fairfield itself has quite a broad, flat, summit, the best views from which are obtained by wandering a little around its edges. In mist keep a check on your compass. Connecting Fairfield to St Sunday Crag is a fairly slender ridge that adds an adventurous quality to the walk but is really none too difficult to negotiate. Finally the walk concludes with a very elevated traverse round Birks Fell from which there are some very impressive views of Grisedale and Ullswater.

1 Pass through the six bar gate a few yards south of the telephone box at Bridge End on to a trackway indicated as being a public right of way. A few hundred yards from the gate a small white waymark arrow on a single post indicates that a right of way, a footpath, veers off to the left from the track to a wooden stile crossing over a stone wall. Over the stone wall the path continues to follow the crest of the ridge ahead of you. The ridge eventually leads to the foot of Hart Crag at which point the path continues up the face of the fell to its summit. (3 miles)

2 From the top of Hart Crag turn right and follow the crest of the ridge on to the summit of Fairfield. (¾ mile)

3 The highest point on Fairfield seems to be a circular shelter from which head towards a second shelter a few yards to the north. From there move out to the left, in a north-westerly direction, skirting round the top of a deep gully leading down into Deepdale. A few yards further in the same direction and you should soon observe a small cairn on the edge of the fell, with a vague path leading towards it. As you walk towards the cairn the path becomes more distinct and soon becomes very worn as it makes a steep descent down a sharp arete to Deepdale Hause, the saddle between Fairfield and St Sunday Crag. From the Hause a distinct path continues along the ridge to the top of St Sunday Crag. (1¼ miles)

4 From the top of St. Sunday Crag continue along the summit ridge of the fell in a north-easterly direction. To begin with the path is none too distinct especially in mist but by keeping as much as you can gauge it to the crest of the ridge a clear path soon develops. Descending to just below two thousand feet the path begins contouring the north-western slopes of Birks Fell. (½ mile)

5 Within a few hundred yards of this more level section of walking the path becomes very ill-defined. It is easy at this point to follow an indistinct pathway that descends downhill to the left. Be sure not to do this however but keep walking straight ahead roughly on the same contour. Passing through a dilapidated wall the path becomes clearer again. Finally, having drawn level with and past Braesteads farm, roughly a thousand foot below in Grisedale valley, the path begins a long steep descent, at the bottom of which it comes to a metal gate and wire fence. (1¼ miles)

6 Do not pass through the gate but here turn right and follow the trackway leading away to your right following the line of the fence. Passing through a kissing gate the track reduces to a pathway that leads to Patterdale Post Office. (¾ mile)

7 On reaching the road turn right and follow it back to the starting point of the walk. (1 mile).

HELVELLYN 3116 feet.

Distance	9 ½ miles
Total Feet of Ascent	3000 feet
Suggested Time	6 ½ hours
Starting Point	Glenridding Car Park (NY 386 170).

It is thought that Helvellyn is the most climbed mountain in the Lake District. This is because it surpasses the magic figure of three thousand feet, which is achieved by only three other peaks in the Lake District, and whilst only the third highest mountain in the Lake District it is somewhat more accessible than the two mountains which are highest and second highest, Scafell and Scafell Pike, and therefore it is climbed more often. The ascent taken in this walk is via Striding Edge, a sharp, dramatic, serrated ridge which is no doubt the most difficult route to the summit, but because of these qualities it has also probably become the most popular route to the summit as well. So whilst this is a dramatic climb it is also likely to be fairly busy.

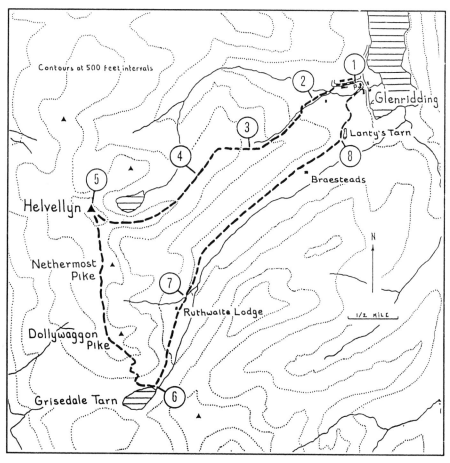

1 From the Information Centre following the footpath direction signs exit the western end of the car park, next to the Health Centre, on to a roadway. Turn left and follow the road uphill. Where the road bends an access road branches off to the left to Gillside Farm. Follow this access road over the bridge and uphill, however do not branch left into the farm but continue uphill to a five bar gate. (½ mile)

2 Continue through the gate and uphill for another hundred yards. At this point branching off to the right is a distinct path signposted as leading to 'Helvellyn via Mires Beck'. Follow this path a few hundred yards uphill to a gate and a stile. Pass through the gate and turn left to continue along the path following Mires Beck. The path climbs steeply uphill eventually joining, at roughly 1700 feet, a solid ridge wall. (¾ mile)

3 The path contiues along the ridge following the wall. After climbing a few hundred feet a dramatic sight of Helvellyn and Catstye Cam comes in to view. There now follows a welcome level section still following the wall to where the wall makes a sharp left hand turn and the path is joined by another path ascending from Grisedale (¾ mile)

4 The path continues along the ridge onto Striding Edge itself. Outside the winter season there is no great difficulty to Striding Edge. The most exciting way to cross it is to keep to the crest of the ridge as much as possible, however there is an easier path, if needed, just below the crest of the ridge on the right hand side. The most difficult part comes where the ridge descends sharply before the final climb to the summit; this is no more than a scramble however and is not too problematical, should it be there is a narrow path to the left that dips and curves around this difficulty starting a few score yards before reaching it. On reaching the summit ridge turn right and walk the last few remaining hundred yards to the summit which is marked with a triangulation pillar. (1¼ miles)

5 From the summit walk south along a very clear ridge path. Half a mile from the summit the path splits in two. Keep to the left hand branch, the higher path, which continues along the ridge. Better views still are obtainable by ignoring the path altogether and walking along the actual edge of the ridge and rejoining the main path at the col between Nethermost Pike and Dollywaggon Pike. Should you do this in winter make sure you are properly equipped. Finally the path descends the southern face of Dollywaggon and links with an old packhourse route near the outflow of Grisedale Tarn. In making this descent try keeping to the original zig-zags of this path; this not only makes the descent easier but also avoids eroding further one of the most eroded paths in the Lake District. (2 miles)

6 Follow the old packhorse route downhill in to Grisedale. After descending 500 feet the path comes to the ruins of Ruthwaite Lodge. A few hundred yards on from these ruins, to your left, is a footbridge which crosses the beck flowing down from Ruthwaite Cove. (1 mile)

7 Cross over the footbridge and follow the path which continues from it contouring along the north-western side of Grisedale valley. After passing above Braesteads Farm the path begins a steady 200 foot climb to Lanty's Tarn. (2½ miles)

8 From Lanty's Tarn an obvious path descends northwards to Glenridding. (½ mile)

Last page ... a solatium?

THE ROMAN ROAD.

Originally I planned to include in this guide a walk from Pooley Bridge to the village of Troutbeck all the way along the course of the Roman Road which crosses the summit of High Street. In the end I decided not to do this as the maps needed to illustrate the walk would take up too much space. However I did prepare the directional notes for this walk and rather than leave this page blank I have decided to reproduce them here as they might be found of some use even without any accompanying maps to anyone considering doing the walk. The walk is roughly 15 miles long and involves about 2500 feet of climbing and should take about 9 hours. In the summer it is possible to return from Troutbeck to Pooley Bridge using the 104 Service bus, operated by Cumberland Motor Services.

Beginning from Pooley Bridge follow the road running along the side of the church signposted as leading to Howtown and Martindale. The road soon forms a cross roads. Continue straight ahead along the road sign posted to Roehead, and also indicated as being a cul-de-sac. Where the road makes a sharp turn left the route to the Roman Road continues straight ahead as a rough trackway signposted as a bridleway leading to Helton over Barton Fell. Eventually, where it begins to level, the trackway reaches a wooden signpost. (1½ miles)

Here turn right and follow the path signposted as a public bridleway to 'Howtown' and the 'Roman Road'. This path almost immediately branches in two. Follow the lefthand branch. Reaching a small stone circle the path again splits in two. This time bear right along the lower more worn branch. Within a few hundred yards, marked with a small cairn, the path splits in two yet again. Bear left. After another few hundred yards for the 'n'th time the path splits again, with a patch of reeds growing between the two branches of the path. Bear left again. For a short distance the path is quite thin then it becomes evident that the ground has been disturbed. As irregular as it is this is the most evident section of the Roman road. Where the gradient of the 'road' eases and becomes almost level there is a cairn of large stones with a taller stone erected in the middle of it. (2½ miles)

From here on the path is very distinct and there is no problem following it all the way on to the summit of High Street, the actual summit of which is set a little away to the east from the course of the Roman Road and is marked by a large white trig point set in the middle of a long dilapidated wall. (6 miles)

From the summit trig point continue to follow the wall southwards. Where the wall makes a sharp righthand turn the path continues straight ahead as a very grassy path. Within a few hundred yards it links up with a broader path descending from Thornthwaite Crag, near to three isolated metal fence posts. About a hundred yards downhill along this broader path, just where it begins to climb uphill, veer off to the right. There is no path, but within a hundred yards of walking across the open fell-side turf you should come upon a very distinct pathway. (1 mile)

This is the course of the Roman Road again. It is a very steep descent and there is little of it that seems like a Roman road. At the foot of the descent the 'road', now simply a footpath, passes through a gate and soon develops into a trackway leading to Troutbeck Park Farm. (2½ miles)

From the farm follow the farm access road. This soon becomes surfaced and is quite long. Eventually it climbs uphill to Troutbeck village. Where it forks bear left. On reaching the main road you will be almost directly opposite the Queen's Head and undoubtedly ready for a drink! (1 ½ miles)